Learn to
DRAW

Drawing
Pirates
and
Pirate
Ships

Jorge Santillan and Sarah Eason

Gareth Stevens
Publishing

Please visit our website, www.garethstevens.com. For a free color catalog of all our high-quality books, call toll free 1-800-542-2595 or fax 1-877-542-2596.

Library of Congress Cataloging-in-Publication Data

Eason, Sarah.
 Drawing pirates and pirate ships / Sarah Eason.
    pages cm. — (Learn to draw)
ISBN 978-1-4339-9545-3 (pbk.)
ISBN 978-1-4339-9546-0 (6-pack)
ISBN 978-1-4339-9544-6 (library binding)
1. Pirates in art—Juvenile literature. 2. Sailing ships in art—Juvenile literature. 3. Drawing—Technique—Juvenile literature. I. Title.
 NC825.P57E27 2013
 743'.87—dc23
                              2012048250

Published in 2014 by
Gareth Stevens Publishing
111 East 14th Street, Suite 349
New York, NY 10003

© 2014 Gareth Stevens Publishing

Produced for Gareth Stevens by Calcium Creative Ltd
Illustrated by Jorge Santillan
Designed by Paul Myerscough
Edited by Rachel Blount

Printed in the United States of America

CPSIA compliance information: Batch CS13GS: For further information contact Gareth Stevens, New York, New York at 1-800-542-2595.

Contents

Learn to Draw!

Many years ago, pirates ruled the seas. They captured ships and stole all their treasure—and sometimes they stole the ship, too! Some pirates sailed in fast ships that could speed across the seas. Others used big ships that were armed with cannons and other weapons. Find out all about pirates and their ships, then learn how to draw them, too.

You will need:

Just a few simple pieces of equipment are needed to create seaworthy drawings of pirates:

Sketchpad or paper
Visit an art store to buy good quality paper.

Pencils
You will need both fine-tipped and thick-tipped pencils.

Eraser
Don't worry if you make a mistake—use an eraser to remove any unwanted lines. You can even use it to add highlights.

Paintbrush, paints, and pens
Buy a set of quality paints, brushes, and coloring pens to add color to your awesome drawings.

Meet the Captain

All pirate ships had a captain. The captain was in charge of the ship and its crew. He gave everyone orders. Pirate captains often designed a pirate flag, which they flew on their ship. The flag was called a "jolly roger."

Step 1

Draw your captain's body, legs, feet, arms, and hands. Then add his head and hat. Draw the shape of the pistol in the right hand and the shape of the sword in the left.

Step 2

Roughly draw the pirate's eyes, nose, ear, and his mustache. Then give your pirate a more rounded outline. Draw the belt, parrot, coat, and boots. Erase the rough lines from step 1.

Step 3

Now add detail to the pirate's face by drawing the eyebrows, nose, ear, mouth, and the shape of the eyes. Draw the fingers. Then add detail to the pirate's clothing, including the buckles on his belt and boots.

Step 4

Now add finer details such as the brim of the hat, the pirate's teeth, the wart on his nose, and the buttons and pockets on his shirt and coat. Add fingernails to his fingers.

Step 5

Add shading to your picture to give it depth. Carefully shade the pirate's face and weapons, then shade his clothes and hat.

Step 6

Give your pirate a bright red coat, purple pants, and a yellow shirt. Color his hat and boots black. Use brown for his beard, eyes, eyebrows, hair, belt, and the handle of his pistol. Add gold buttons and buckles, and a bright blue sword.

Step 7

Now add highlights to the pirate's face, clothes, and weapons. He is ready for action, me hearties!

You're Fired!

If a crew didn't like their captain or felt he was not leading them well, they could vote for a new one! The captain was then forced to leave the ship and his crew.

Ready for Battle

Some pirates sailed in large ships that had up to 30 big cannons. These ships were called "man-of-war" ships. The top decks of the ship carried the cannons. Beneath the top decks were cabins in which the captain and his crew lived.

Step 1

Draw the shape of the ship's base then draw three tall masts. Add the pole at the front of the ship, too. Draw the shape of the sails.

Step 2

Go over your lines from step 1 to give the sails a curved edge. Draw squarish shapes at the top of the masts. Add the markings on the side of the ship. Erase any rough lines from step 1.

Step 3

Add detail by drawing the guns, windows, lantern, and rigging. These are the ropes between the sails and the masts of the ship. Add the flags to the top of the masts.

Step 4

Add more detail to the guns and the front of the ship. Draw the waves around the ship's hull.

Step 5

Carefully shade the base of the ship and the waves. Then add shading to the mast and the sails, too.

Step 6

Color the base of the ship brown. Use cream for the edges of the ship and the sections of the hull. Color the sails cream and use blue for the guns and the windows. Color the lantern gray and yellow. Use dark brown for the flags.

Surrender or Die!

If a treasure ship did not surrender to a pirate crew at once, the pirates would sail close enough to jump onto the ship. They then fought the crew until they handed over all the treasure on board their ship, and often the ship, too.

Step 7

Now add highlights to your pirate ship's sails and the hull. Add highlights to the flags on top of the masts, so they seem to flutter in the wind. Your pirate ship is seaworthy and ready for a treasure hunt!

Hand It Over!

Pirates stole gold, jewels, and even food and weapons from ships they captured. Most pirates quickly spent any money they stole and sold their treasure. When a pirate crew captured a ship, they divided its treasure up between themselves.

Step 1

Draw your pirate's sturdy body. Then draw his legs, feet, arms, and hand and hook. Add his head and a large box for the treasure chest next to him.

Step 2

Go over the lines from step 1 to give the pirate a curved outline. Roughly mark the features on his face and draw his bandana. Add detail to the hand and hook, then pencil the lid of the treasure chest and the outline of the treasure inside it.

Step 3

Draw the shape of the pirate's eyes, mouth, mustache, nose, and pointed beard. Add his shirt, waist sash, the knife inside it, and the ragged edge of his pants. Draw his fingers and toes, then add the treasure in the chest.

Step 4

Bring your pirate to life by drawing his jewelry, ear, teeth, and the rest of his beard. Add hairs to his arms, stripes on his shirt, and the patch on his pants. Add detail to the knife and treasure, too.

Step 5

Add shading to your picture to give it depth and drama. Shade the pirate's body and clothes, then add shading to the treasure chest, too.

Step 6

Give your pirate a red bandana and waist sash. Color his pants green and his shirt blue and white. Use brown for his eyes and hair, and give him white teeth. Color the treasure chest brown and use yellow for the glittering gold!

Step 7

Add the beige-colored spots on the bandana and the highlights on the pirate's body and clothes. Don't forget to add highlights to the gold, too. Now, where would *you* bury the treasure?!

Where's the Treasure?

Some pirates buried their treasure in chests. One of the most famous of pirate captains, Captain William Kidd, is said to have buried 100,000 gold coins. It is believed that he buried them somewhere along the east coast of the United States, but the treasure has never been found!

Speedy Sloops

Some pirates sailed small, light ships that could easily catch a larger ship weighed down with treasure. Small pirate ships were also easy to hide in inlets and creeks along the coast. One-mast pirate ships were called sloops.

Step 1

Draw the base of your ship. Add the mast and the pole at the front of the ship. Then draw squares and triangles for the sails and flag.

Step 2

Go over the sail and flag lines to give them a curved outline. Do the same to the hull of the ship. Add the lines of the waves.

Step 3

Now add detail to the shape of the hull. Then draw the rigging, too.

Step 4

Add the plank marks on the ship's hull and the "jolly roger" flag pattern. Add the markings on the sails and the detail of the water around the ship.

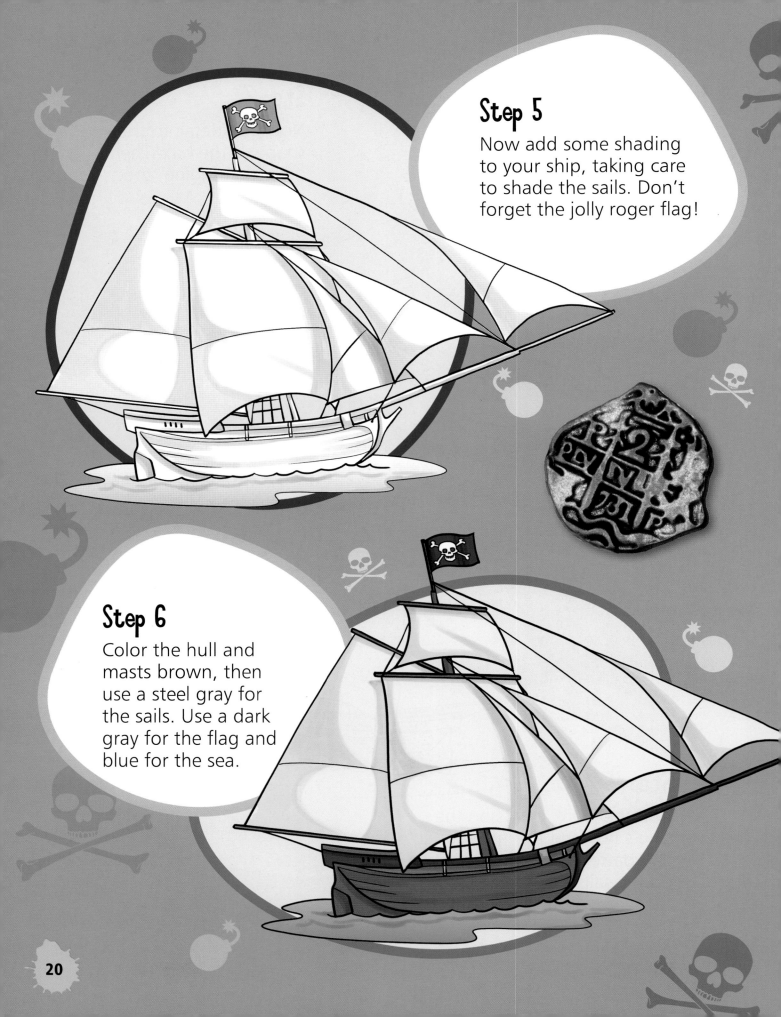

Step 5

Now add some shading to your ship, taking care to shade the sails. Don't forget the jolly roger flag!

Step 6

Color the hull and masts brown, then use a steel gray for the sails. Use a dark gray for the flag and blue for the sea.

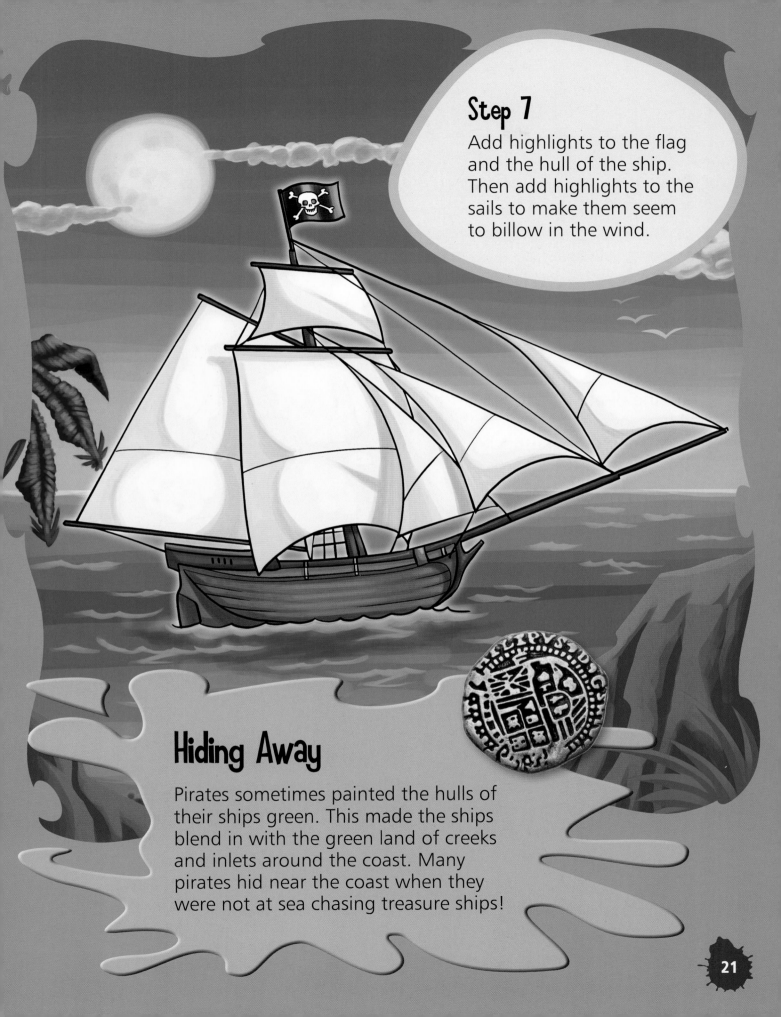

Step 7

Add highlights to the flag and the hull of the ship. Then add highlights to the sails to make them seem to billow in the wind.

Hiding Away

Pirates sometimes painted the hulls of their ships green. This made the ships blend in with the green land of creeks and inlets around the coast. Many pirates hid near the coast when they were not at sea chasing treasure ships!

Peg-leg Pirates

Pirate battles were deadly. Pirates fought with swords called cutlasses, pistols, and axes. Once a pirate crew had taken control of a treasure ship, they often forced its crew to "walk the plank" into the sea!

Step 1

Draw the pirate's body, leg, peg leg, foot, arms, and hands. Then draw his neck and head. Add the swords.

Step 2

Go over the rough lines from step 1 to create a finer outline. Mark the eyes and nose, and draw the pirate's headscarf, hair, and hands. Add the shape of his shirt and pants.

22

Step 3

Now add lots of detail. Give your pirate a mustache, earring, and an eyepatch. Add his belts and waist sash. Put a buckle on his shoe and add detail to his hair.

Step 4

Draw the teeth, spots on the pirate's face, and buttons on his shirt. Add detail to the hair, belts, fingers, and peg leg.

Step 5

Shade your pirate to bring out his features and add depth to his clothing. Carefully shade his weapons, too.

Step 6

Now add color. Use a bright green for the bandana, brown for the hair, peg leg, belt, and sword handles. Color the shirt gray, the pants red, and the waist sash blue. Add gold for the buckles and earring.

Step 7

Add the stripes on the pirate's shirt and peg leg. Then add highlights for the final detail. Your pirate is ready for battle!

Patching Up Pirates

Sometimes pirates lost a leg, hand, or even an eye in a fight. If this happened, the ship's doctor might make the pirate a false wooden leg or a wooden hook. Many pirates wore patches to cover up an eye damaged in battle.

Schooner Sailors

Some pirates sailed in two-mast ships, called schooners. The sailors on board a pirate ship had to wash the decks, mend the sails, cook, clean, and repair any damage to the ship caused during battle. A pirate ship had to be well maintained and ready for action at all times!

Step 1

Draw the base of your schooner, then the tall masts. Add the shape of the ship's sails.

Step 2

Give the sails a curved outline, then add the rigging and the markings on the prow and the hull.

Step 3

Add some more detail to the base of the ship. Draw a lantern at the ship's stern and the waves beneath the hull.

Step 4

Now add lots of detail to the rigging and the markings on the sails. Draw the flag at the rear of the ship and the plank marks on the hull.

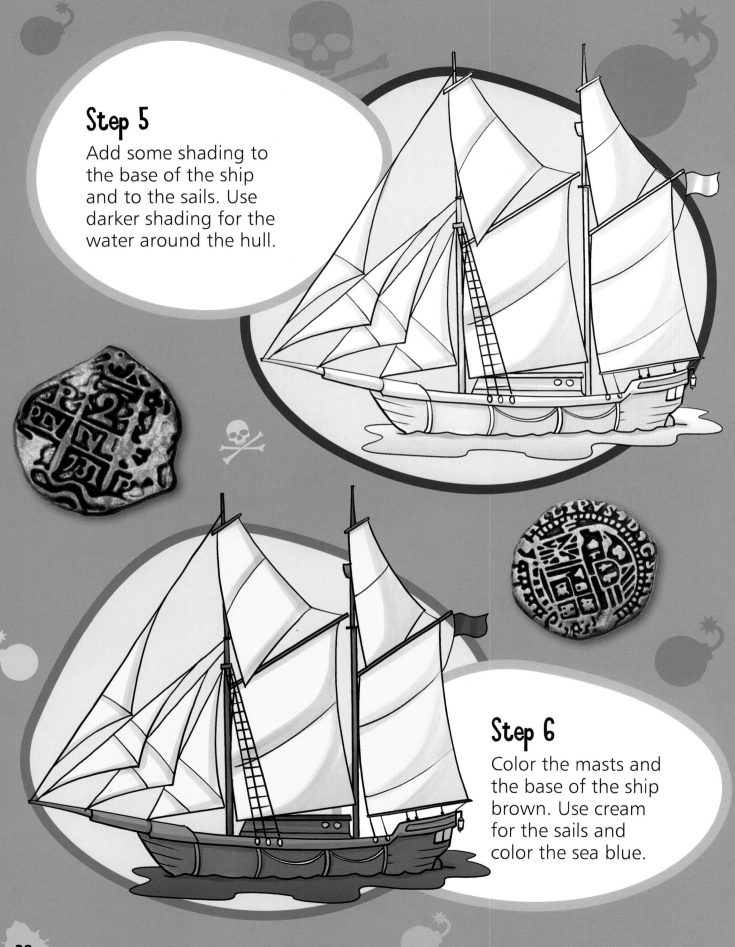

Step 5

Add some shading to the base of the ship and to the sails. Use darker shading for the water around the hull.

Step 6

Color the masts and the base of the ship brown. Use cream for the sails and color the sea blue.

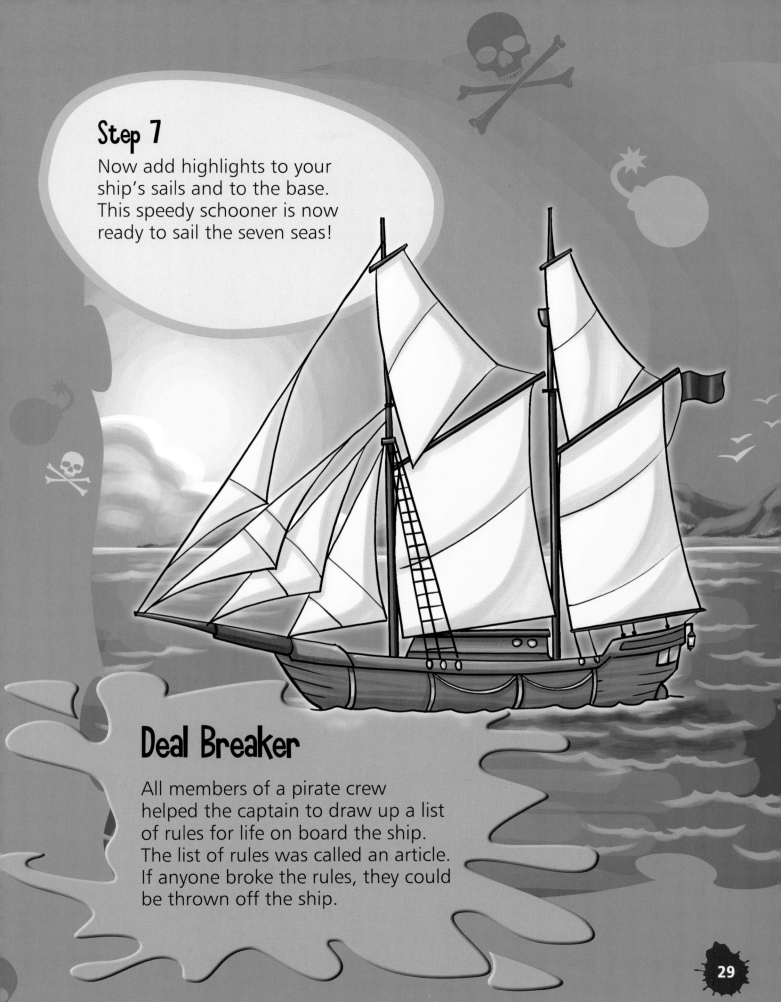

Step 7

Now add highlights to your ship's sails and to the base. This speedy schooner is now ready to sail the seven seas!

Deal Breaker

All members of a pirate crew helped the captain to draw up a list of rules for life on board the ship. The list of rules was called an article. If anyone broke the rules, they could be thrown off the ship.

Glossary

cabins the rooms inside a ship or boat

cannons large guns that fired heavy metal balls called cannonballs

captain the person who is in charge on a ship

captured to take control of something or someone

creeks a natural stream of water smaller than a river

crew a group of people who work together

damaged to have caused harm

deadly very dangerous, can kill

decks the levels of a ship or boat

detail the fine lines on a drawing

divided separated into parts

erase to remove

features the eyes, eyebrows, nose, and mouth of a face

highlights the light parts on a picture

hulls the sides of a ship or boat

inlets narrow waterways

maintained looked after

mast a tall pole on a ship or boat. The mast holds up the sails.

orders instructions that a person must follow

patches pieces of fabric that are worn over an injured eye or sewn onto clothing to cover a hole or tear

pistols small guns

repair to mend

sailors people who sail boats or ships

shading the dark markings on a picture

stern the rear of a ship

surrender to give up

vote to help to decide something

walk the plank when a person is forced to walk along a narrow wooden board from a ship so that they fall into the ocean below

weapons equipment used to fight, such as swords and guns

For More Information

Books

Antram, David. *How to Draw Pirates*. New York, NY: PowerKids Press, 2011.

McCleay, Rob. *Pirate Arrrt!: Learn to Draw Fantastic Pirates, Treasure Chests, Ships, Sea Monsters and More*. Berkeley, CA: Ulysses Press, 2008.

Soloff-Levy, Barbara. *How to Draw Pirates: Captain, Crew, Ships & More*. Mineola, NY: Dover Publications, 2008.

Websites

Find out more about the greatest pirates to ever live at:
webtech.kennesaw.edu/jcheek3/pirates

Discover more about the world of pirates and the rules by which they lived at:
www.thekidswindow.co.uk/News/Pirates.htm

Read about pirate adventures, treasure maps, sea songs and much more at:
www.rochedalss.eq.edu.au/pirates

Index

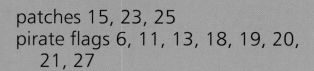